THIS BOOK BELONGS TO:

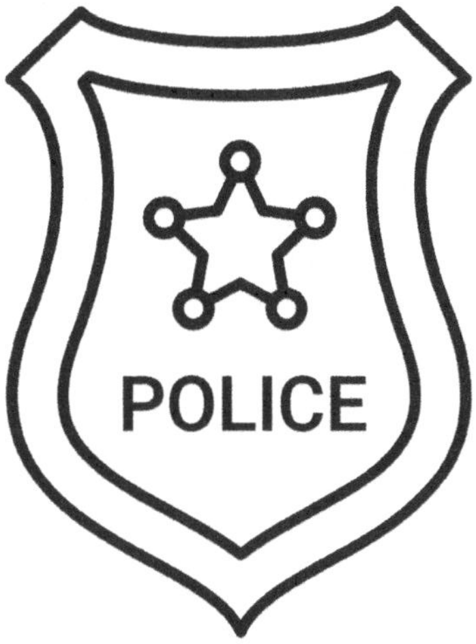

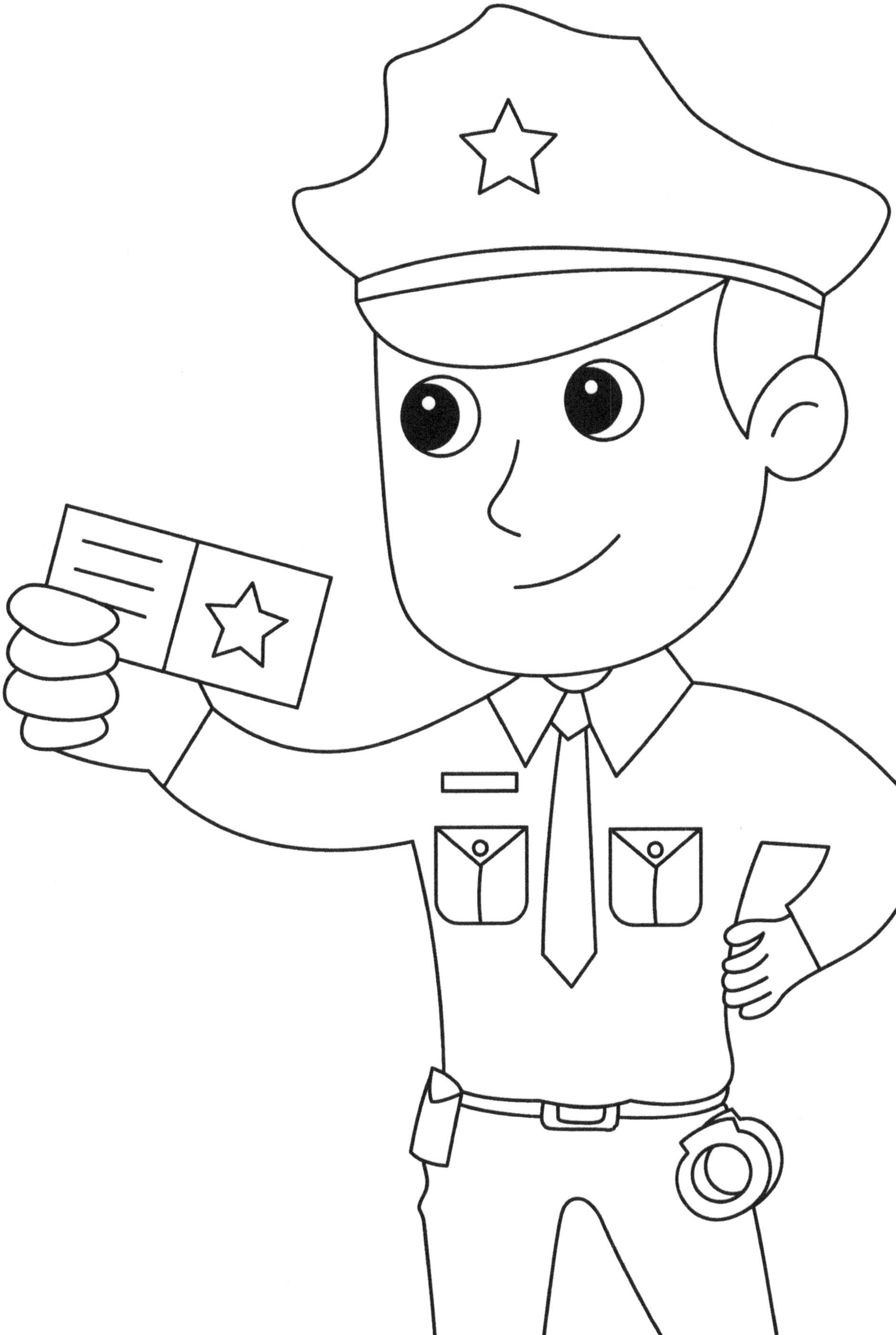

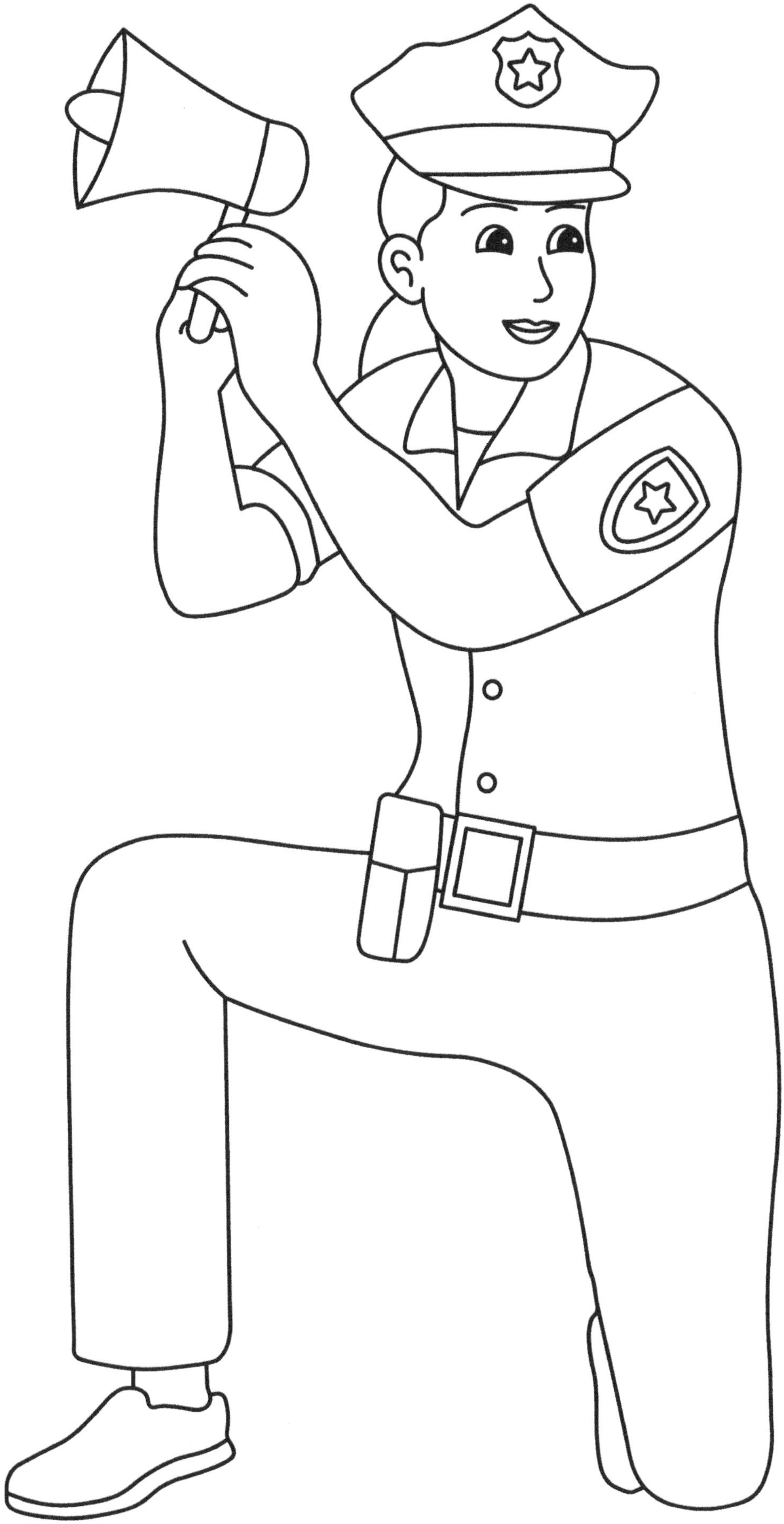

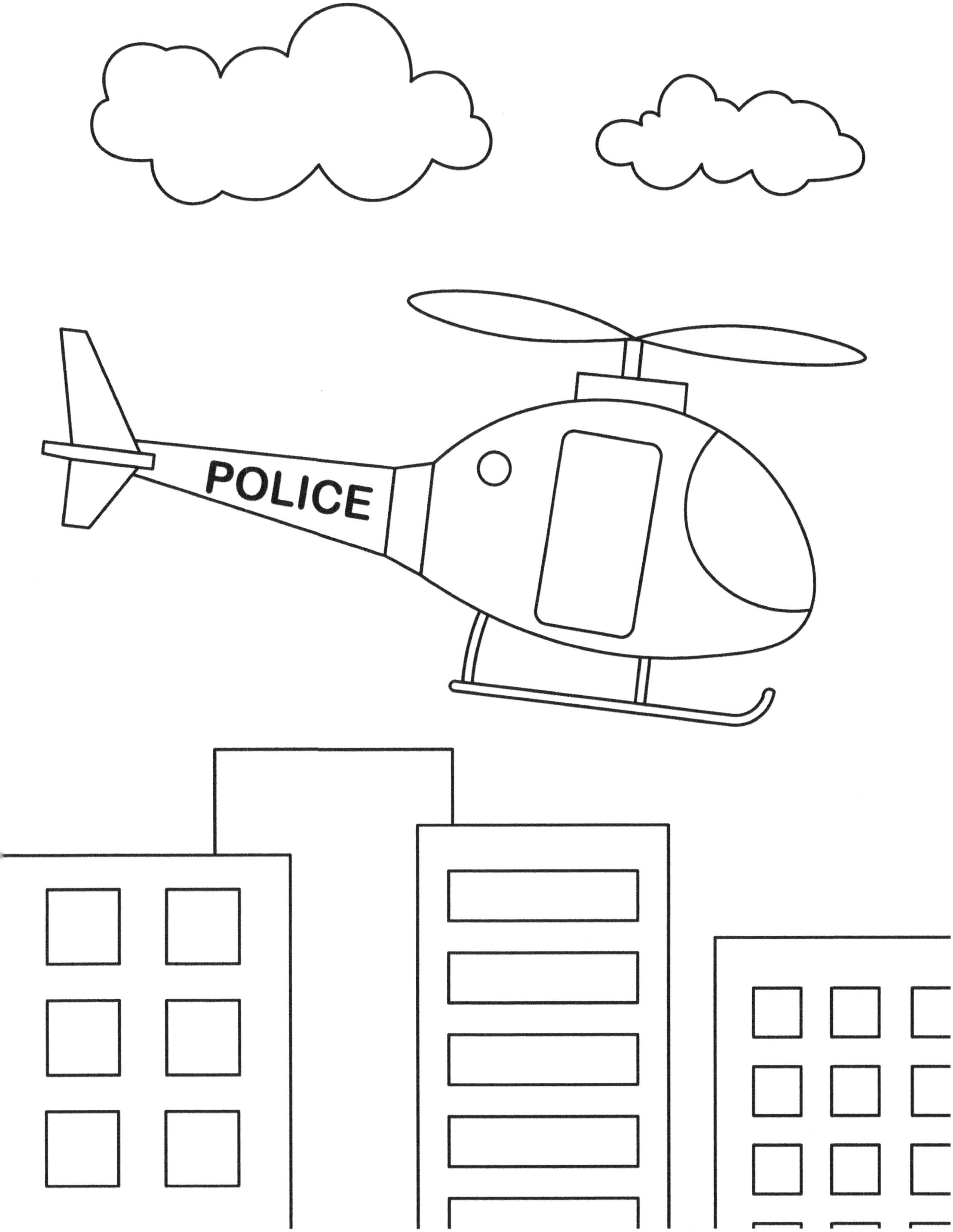
POLICE

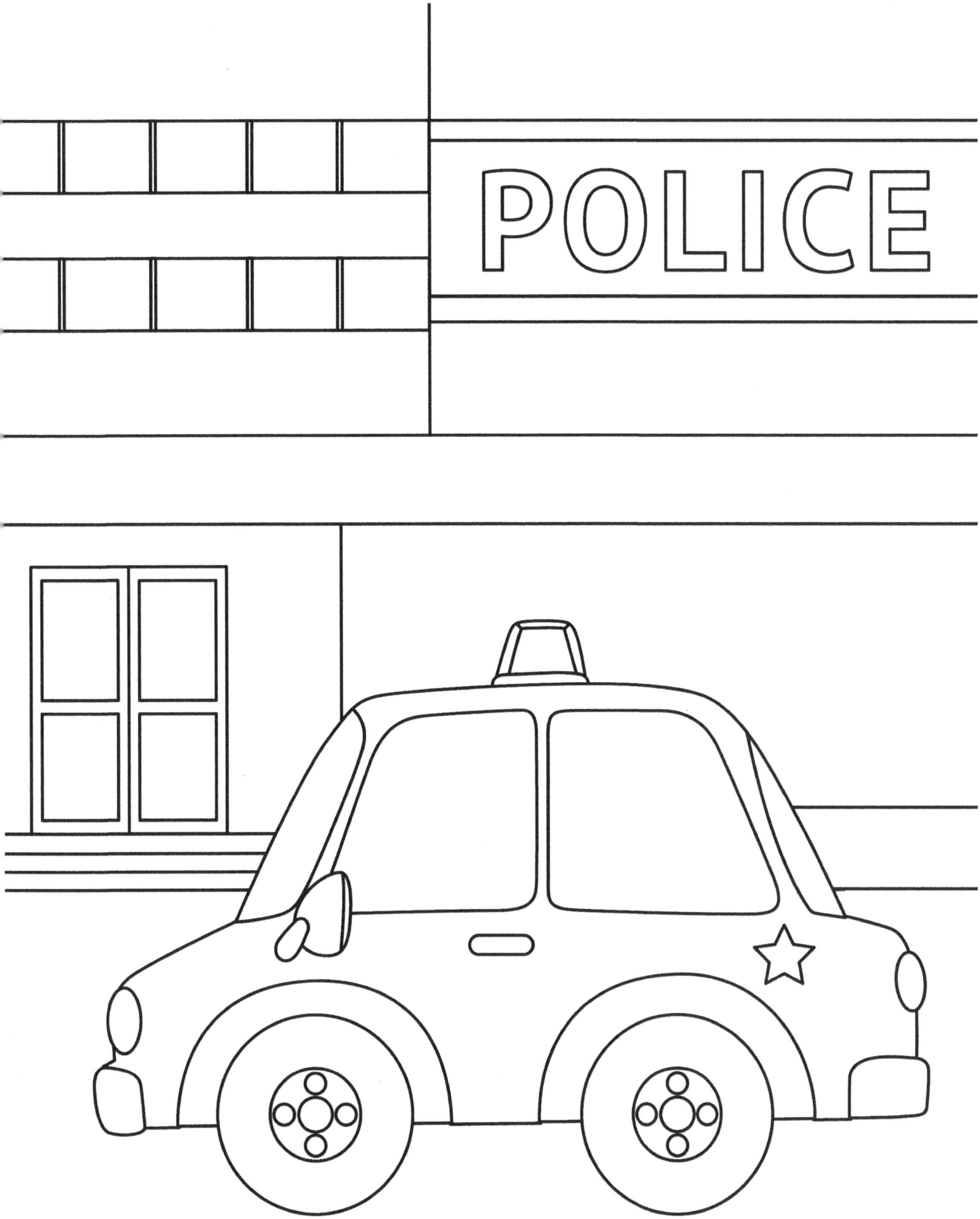
POLICE

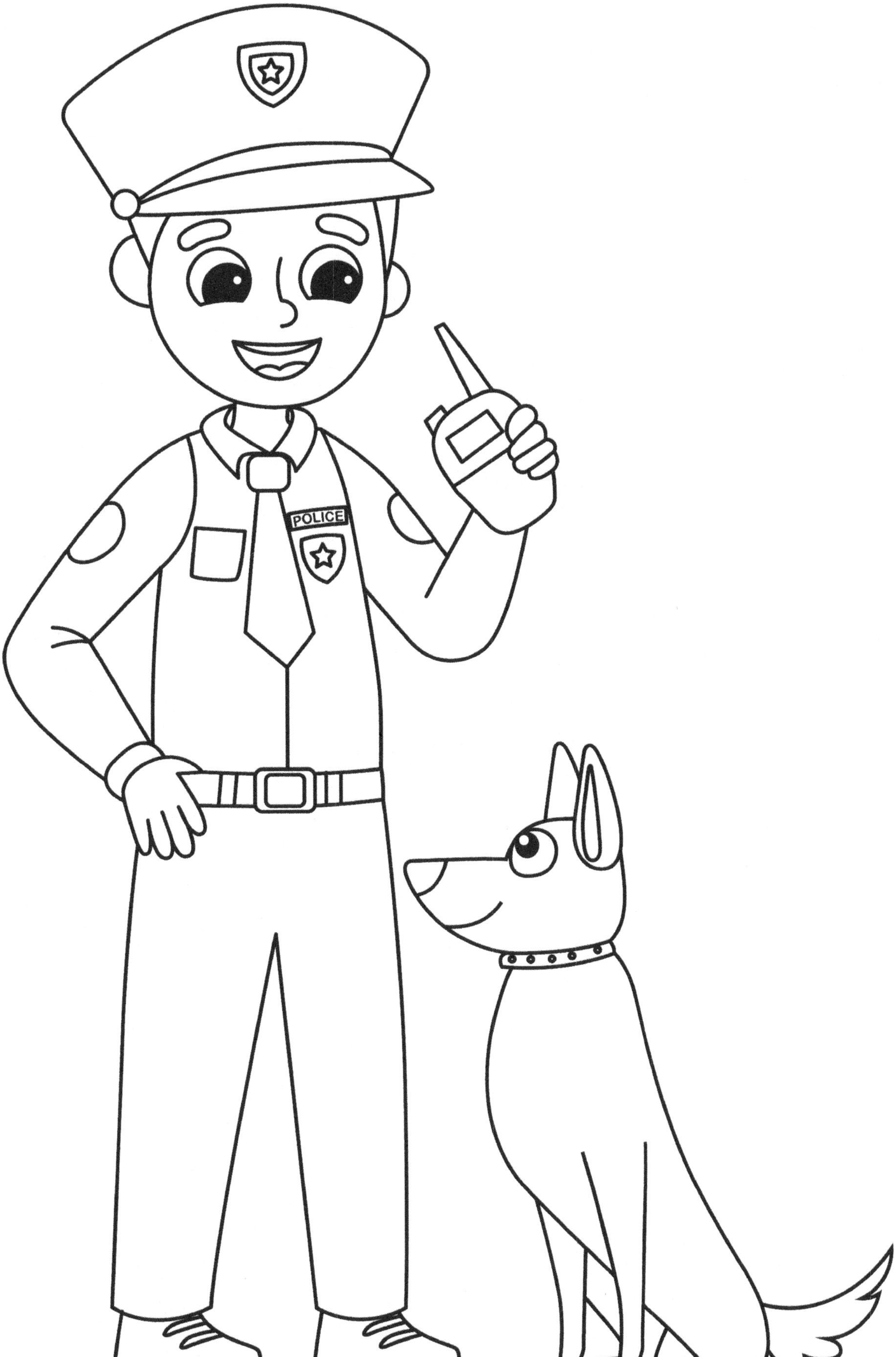
POLICE

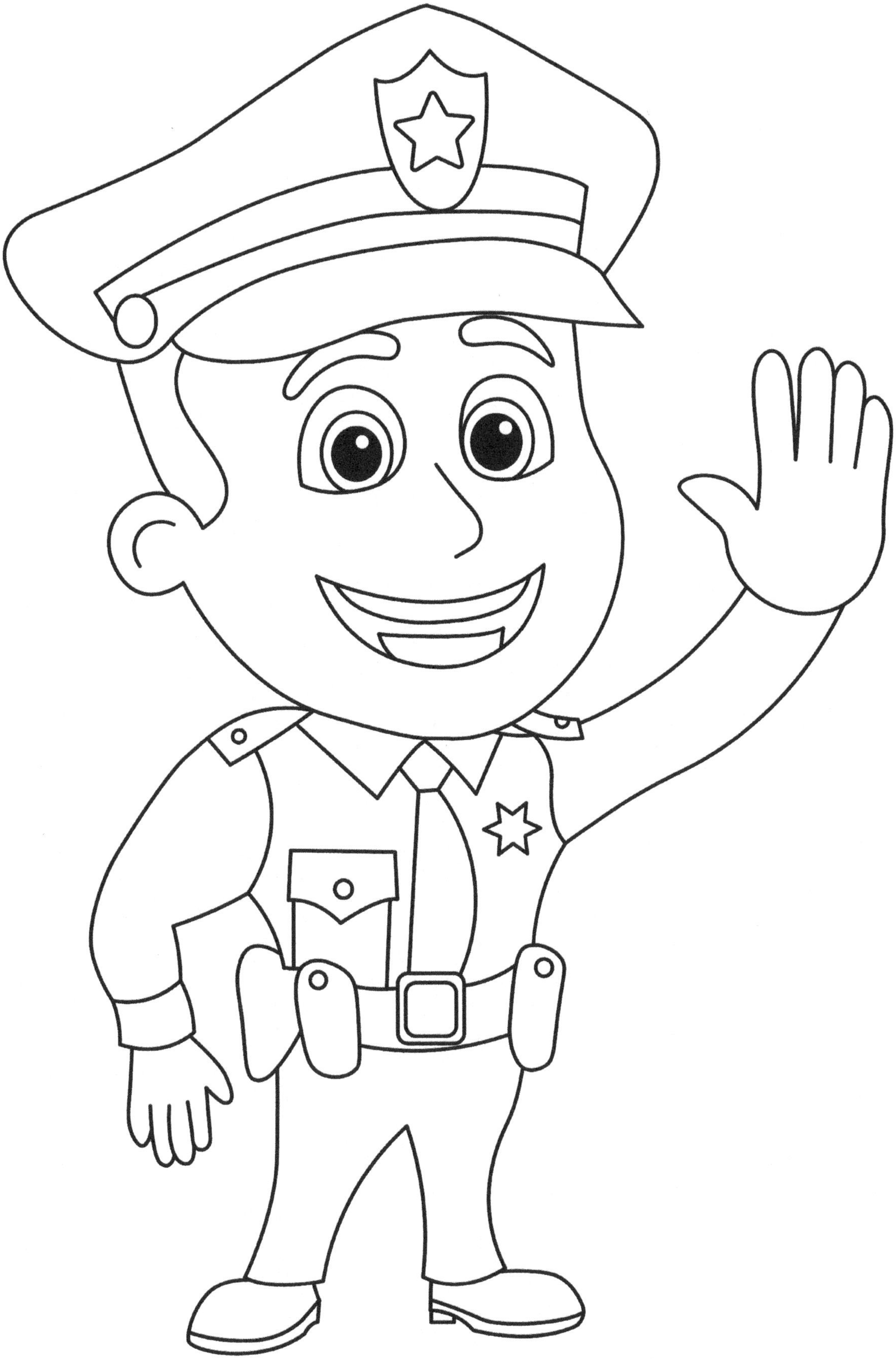

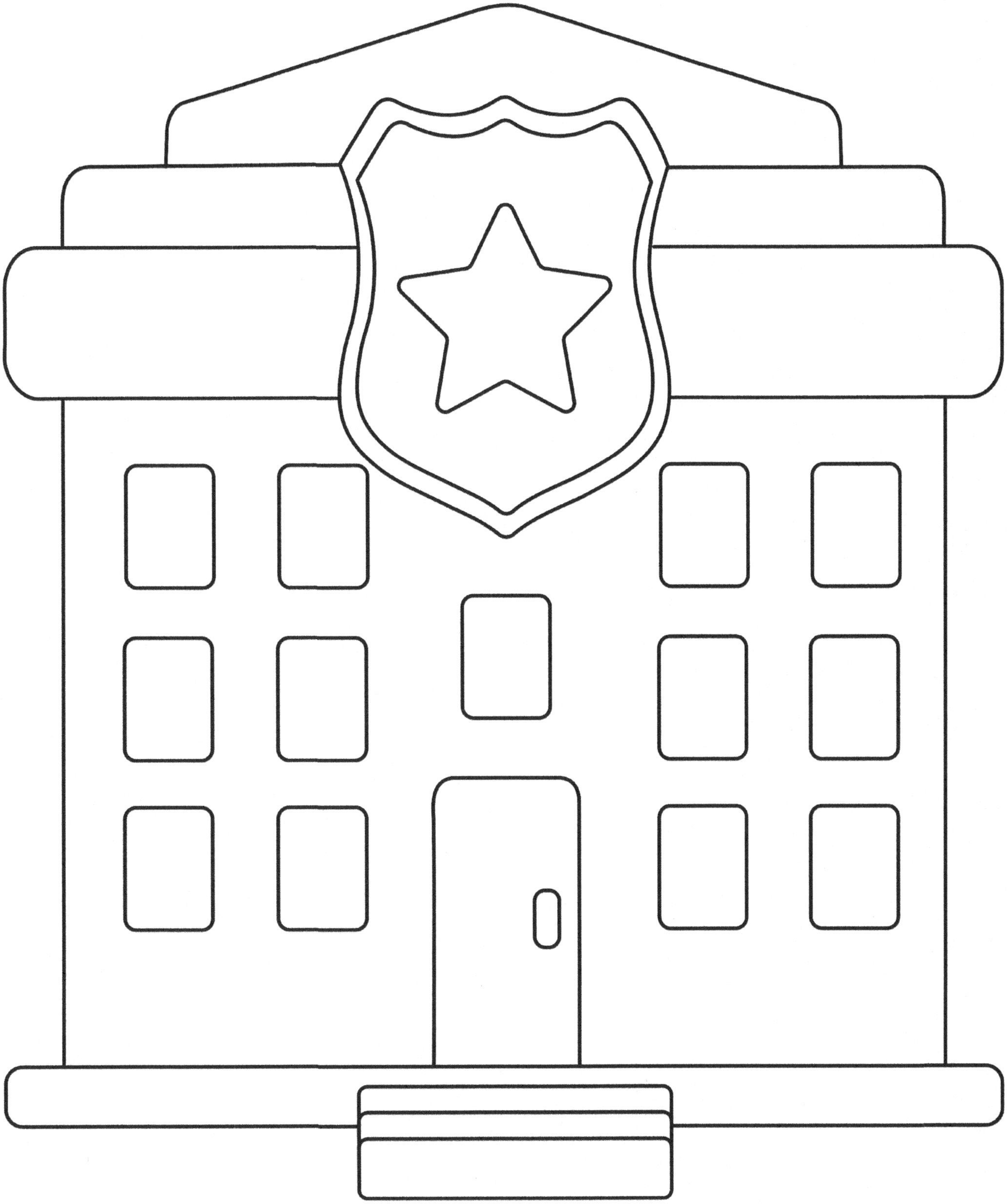

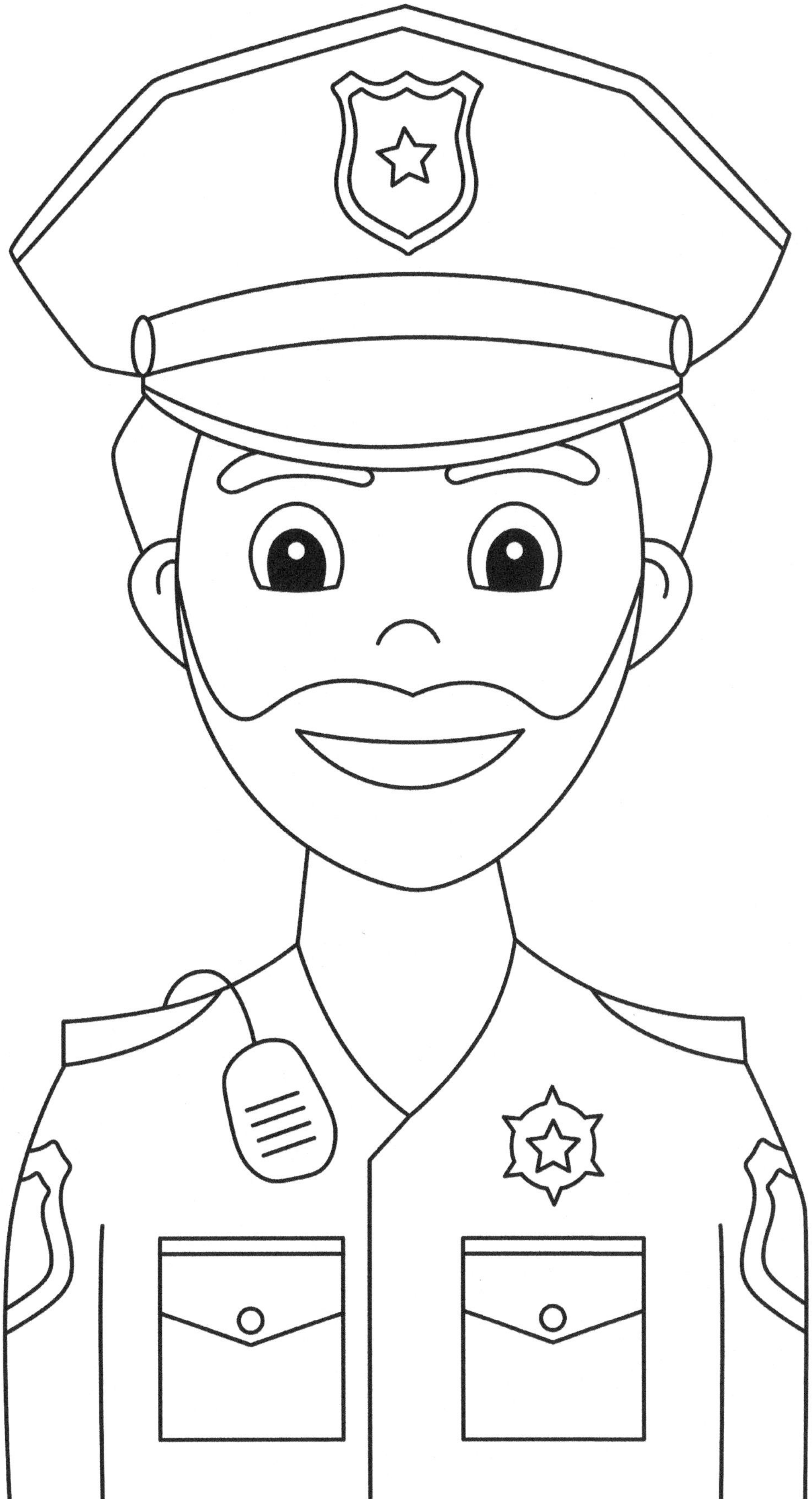

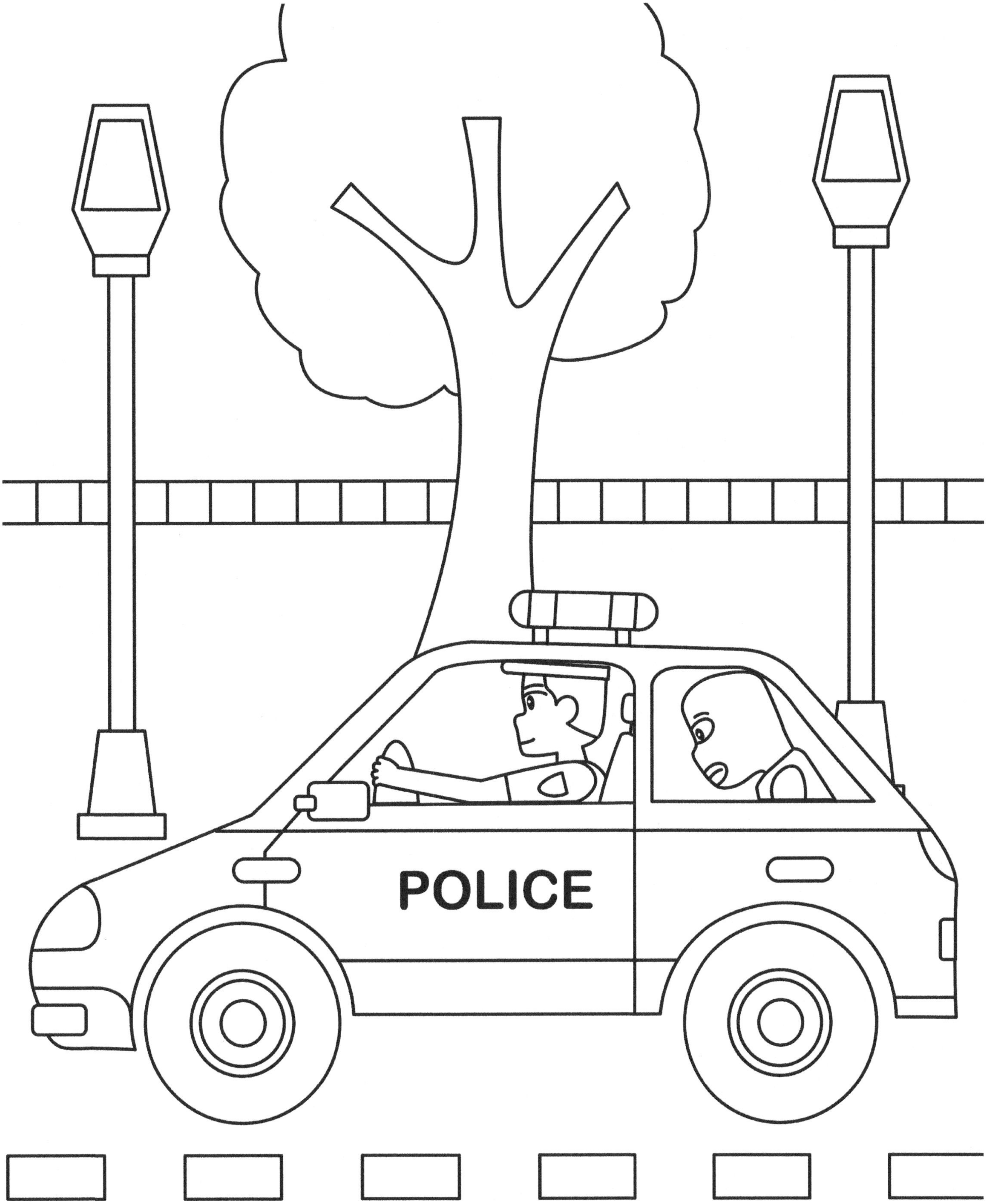
POLICE

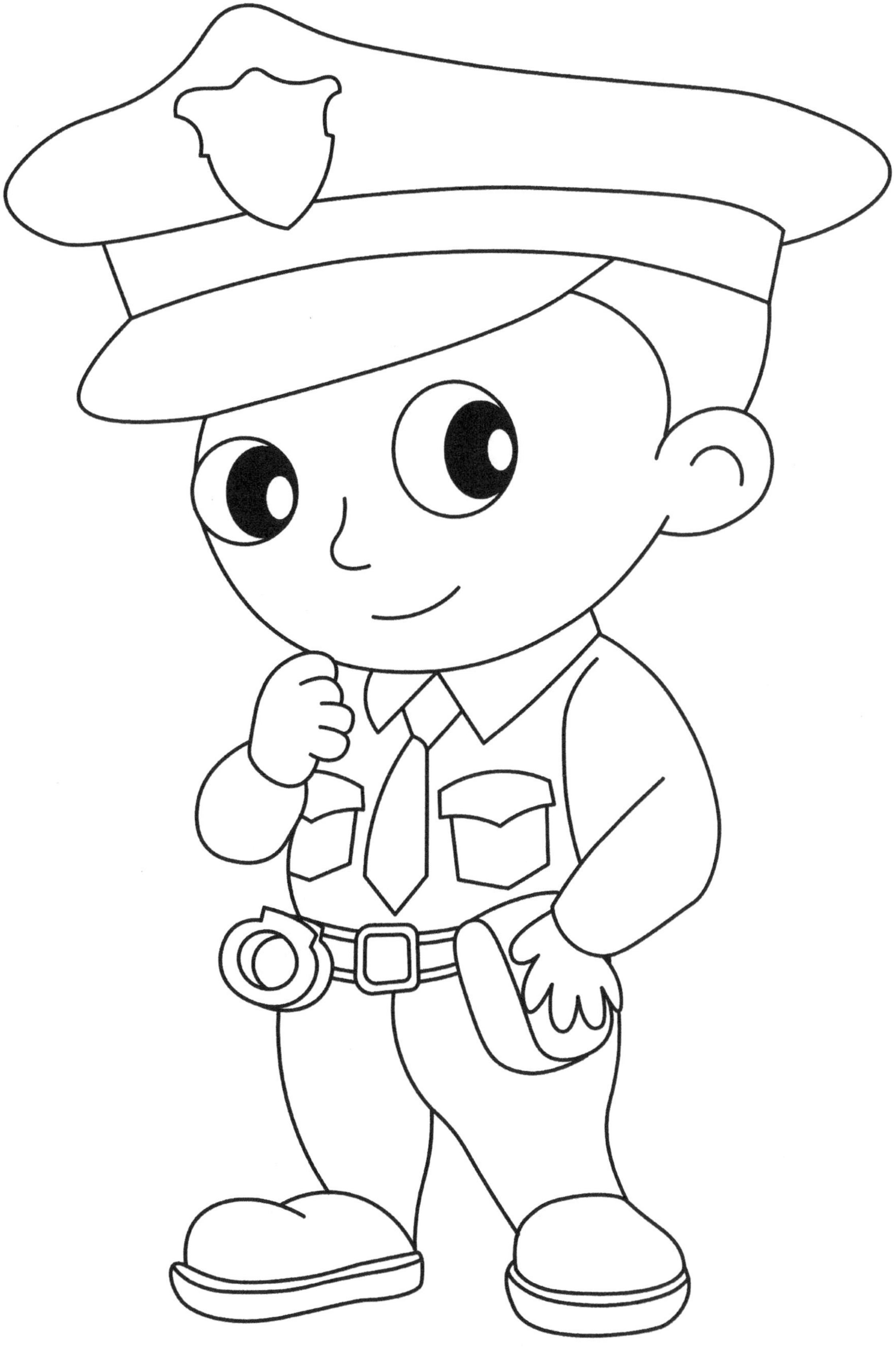

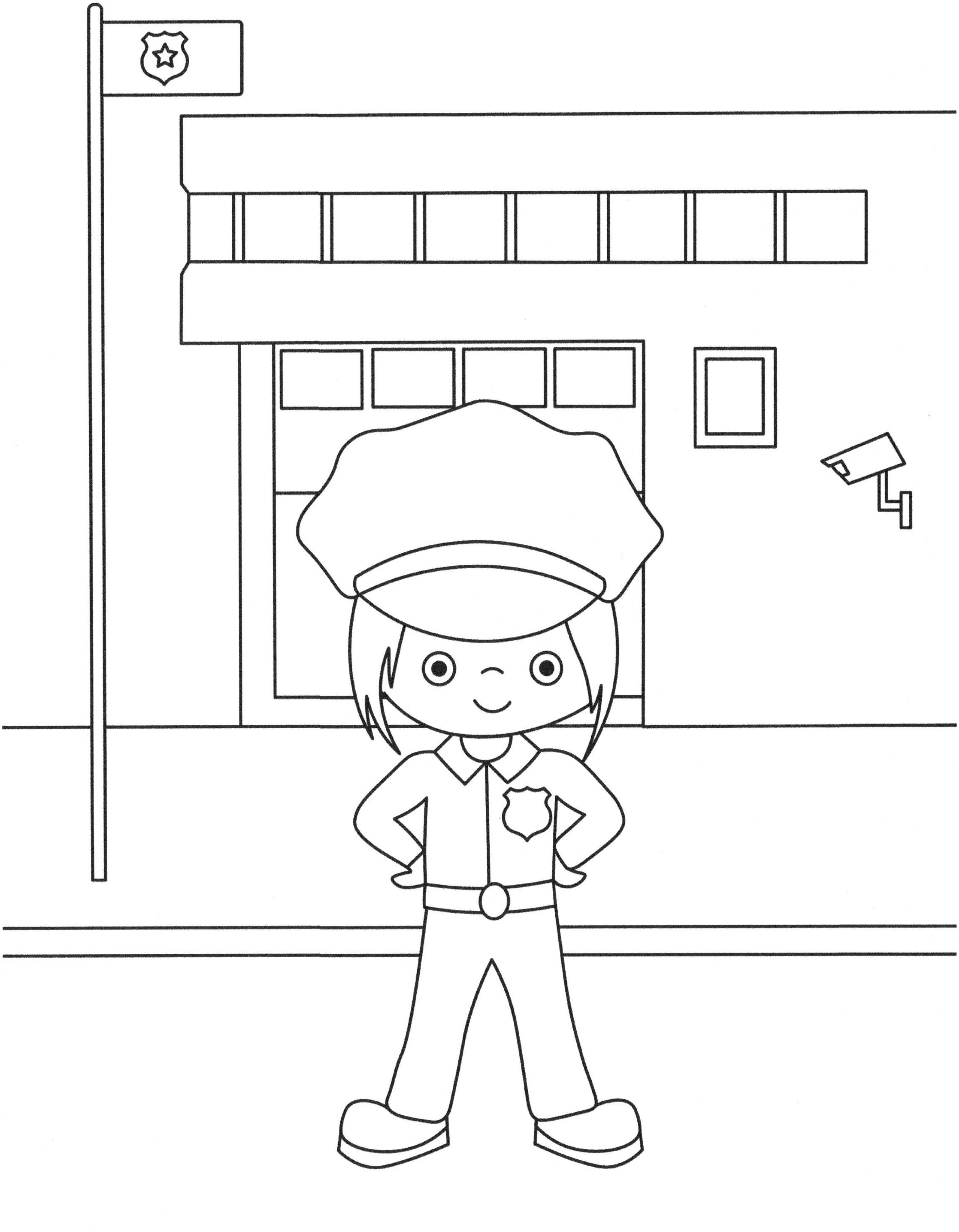

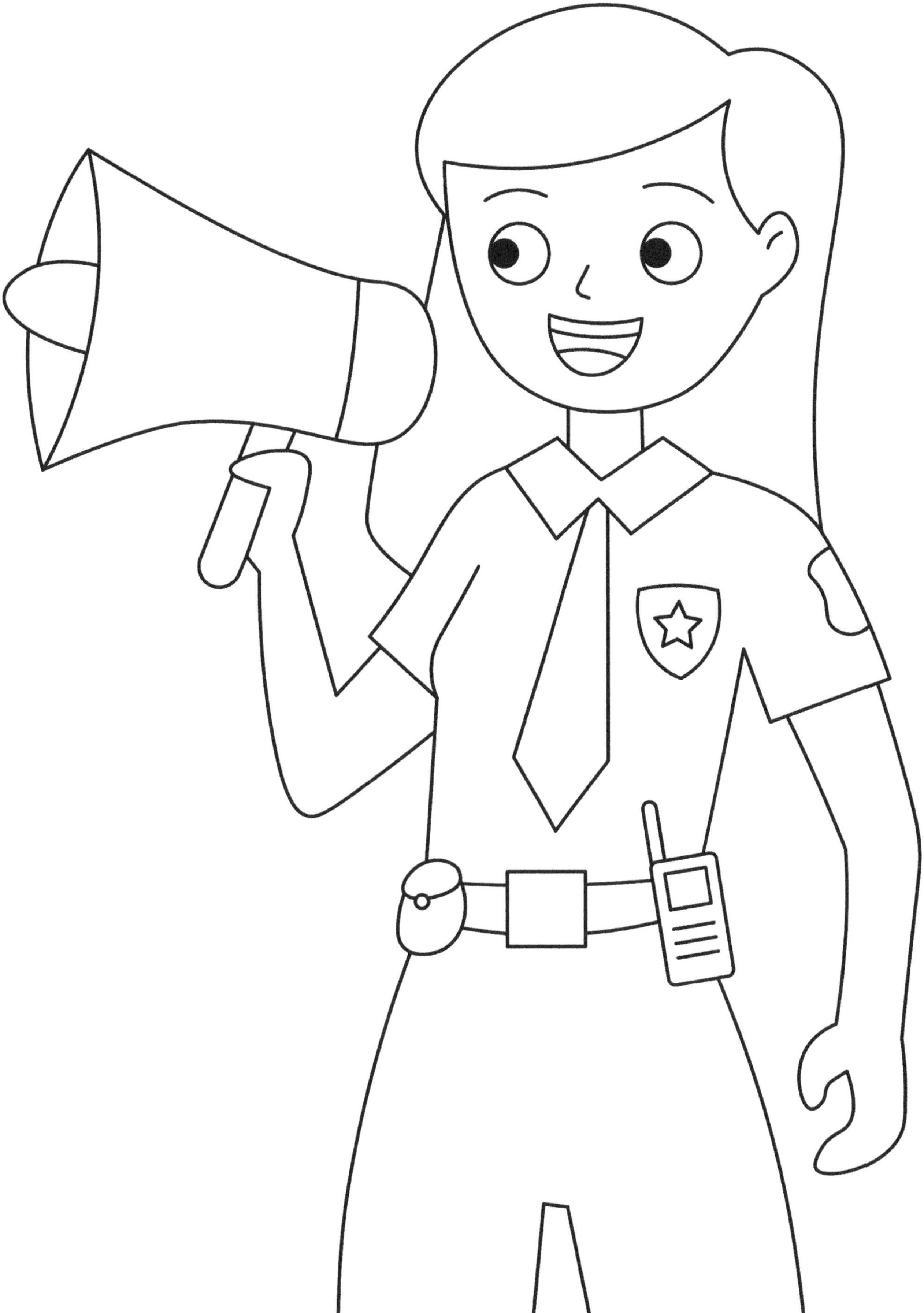

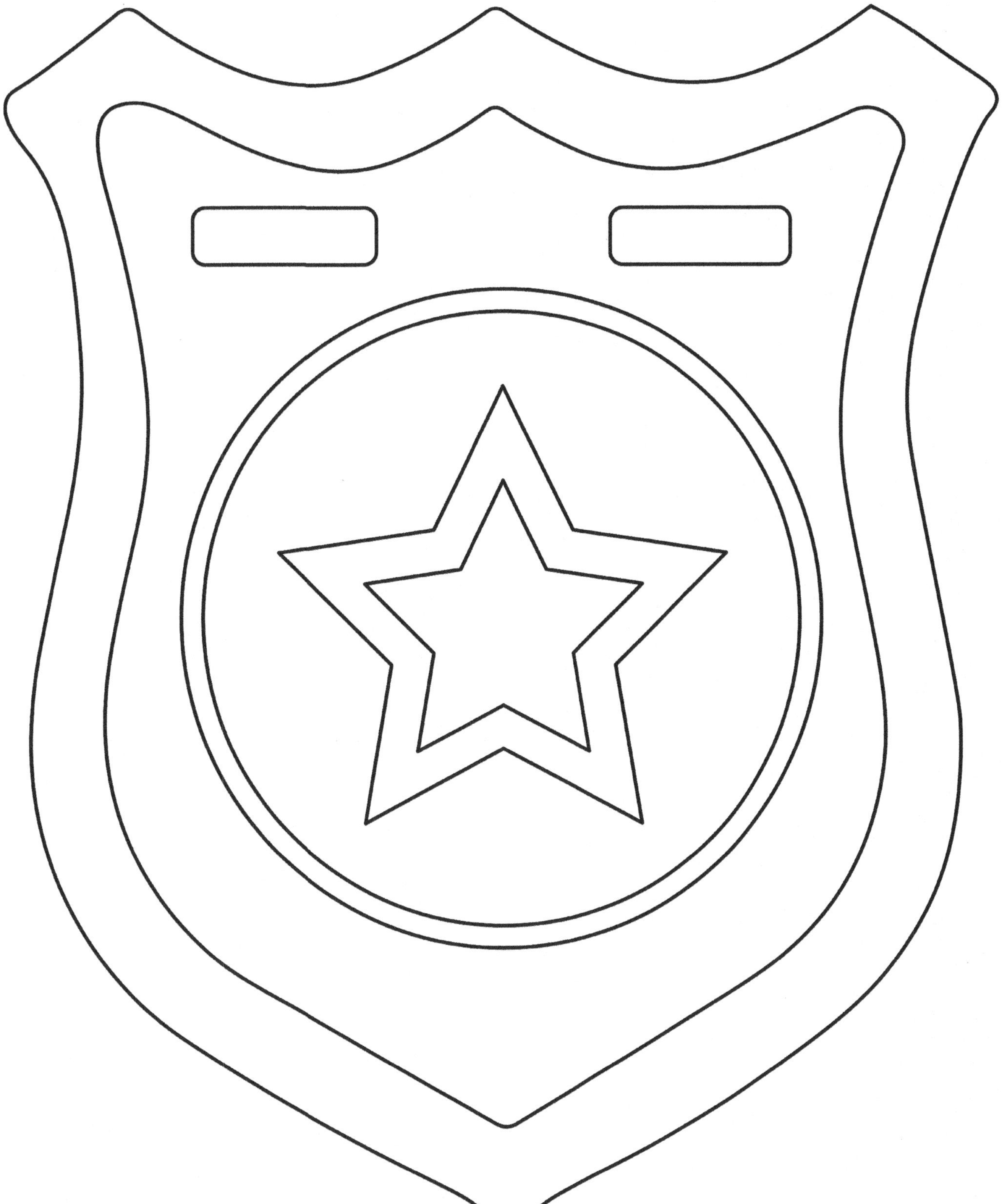

WANTED

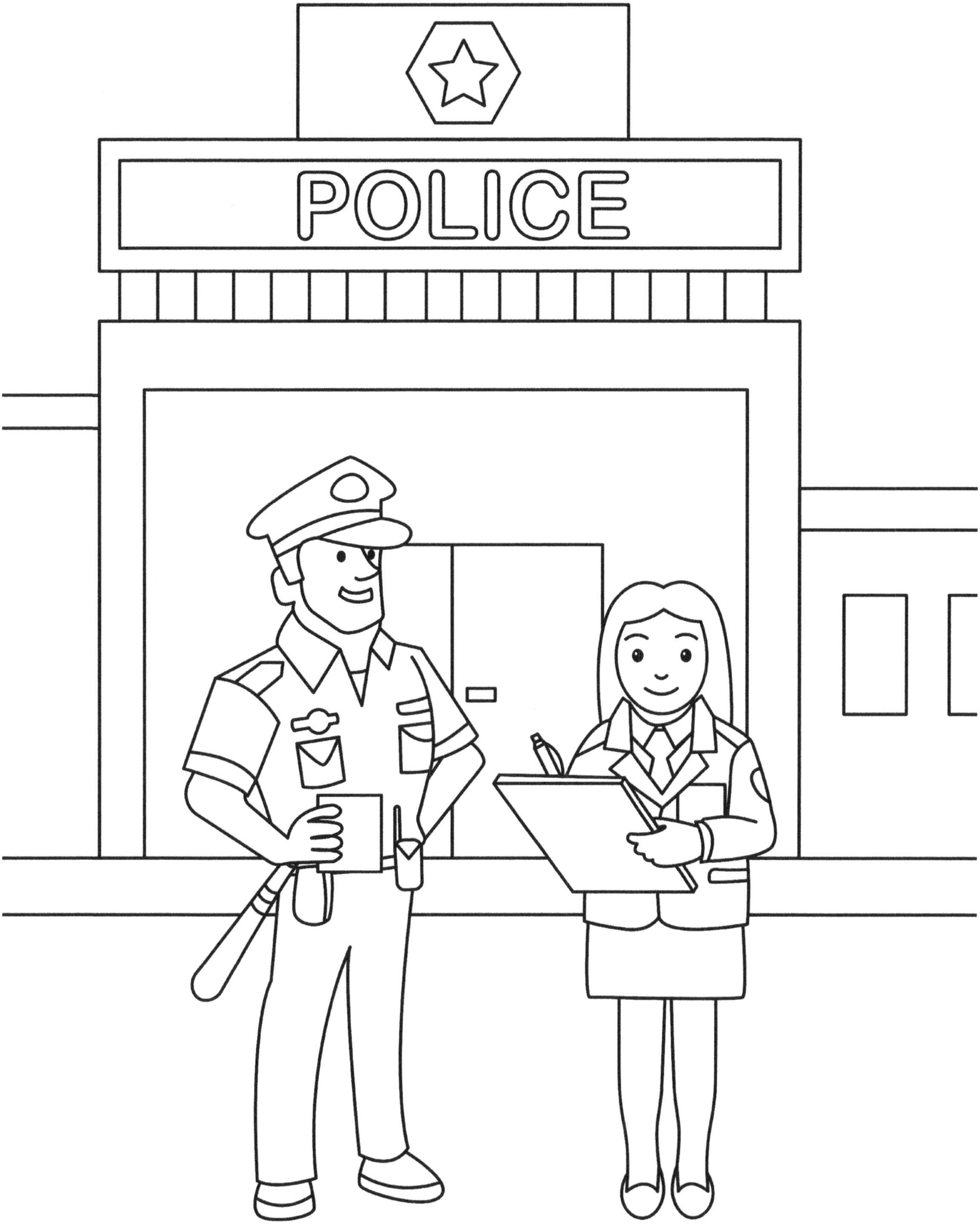
POLICE

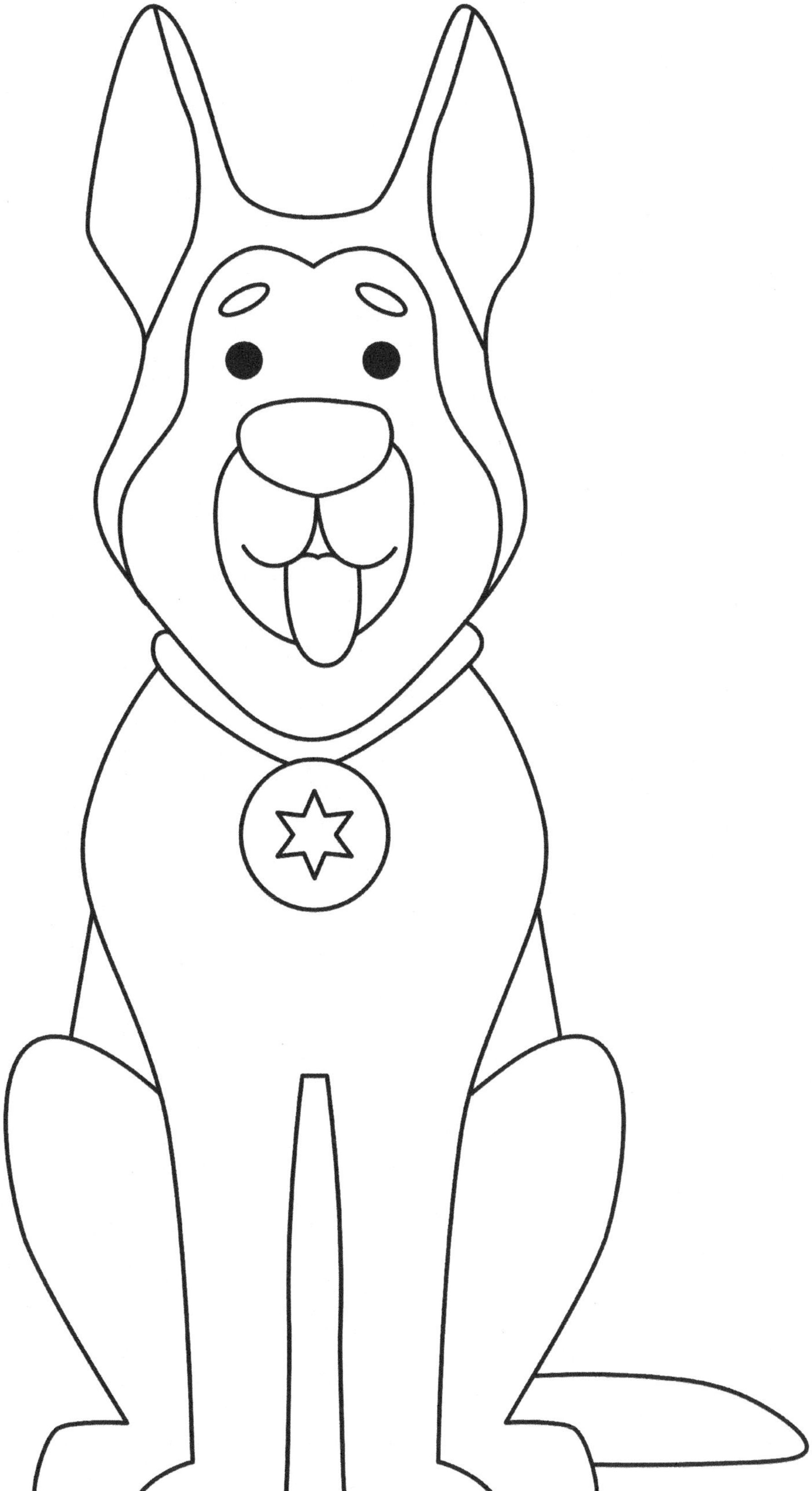

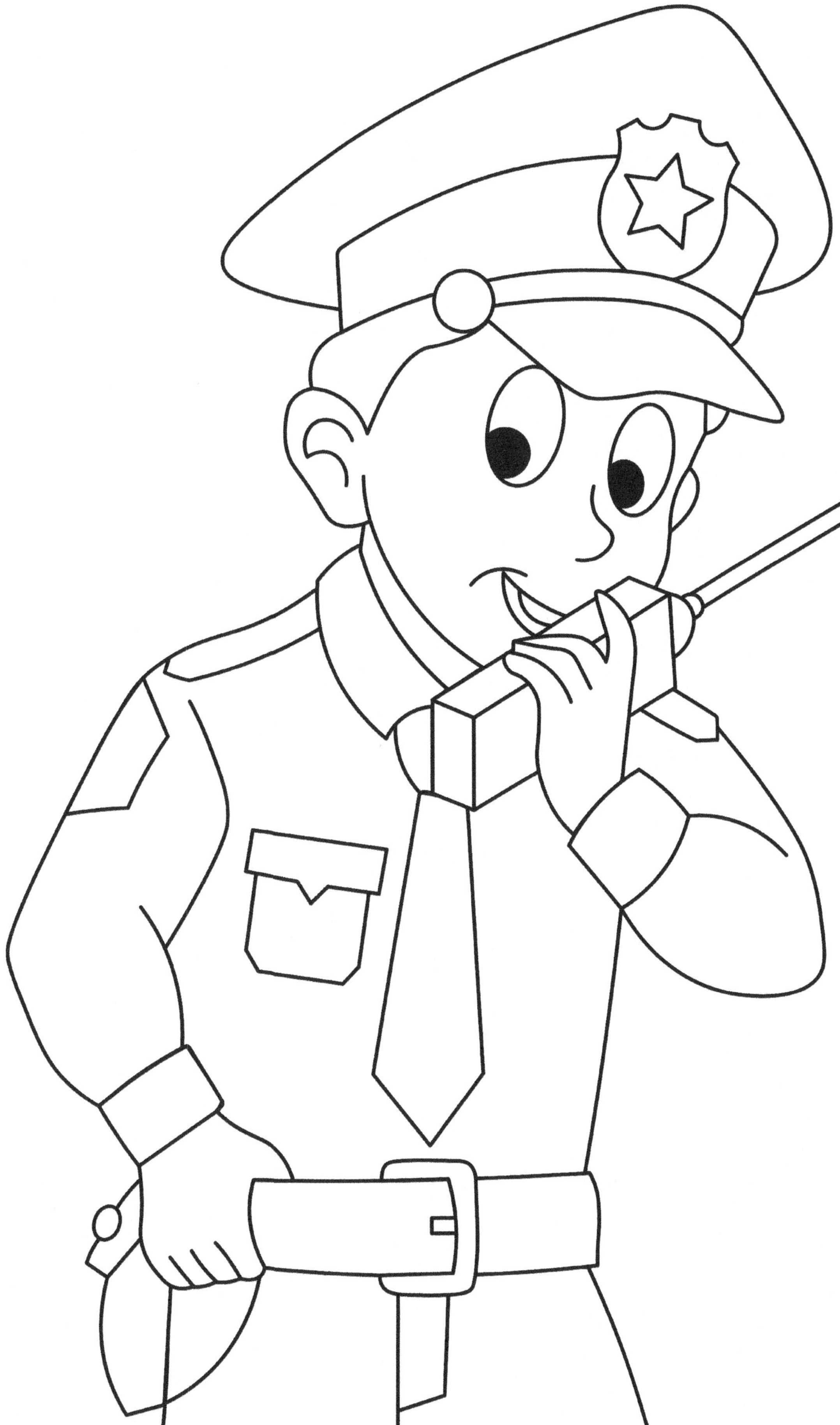

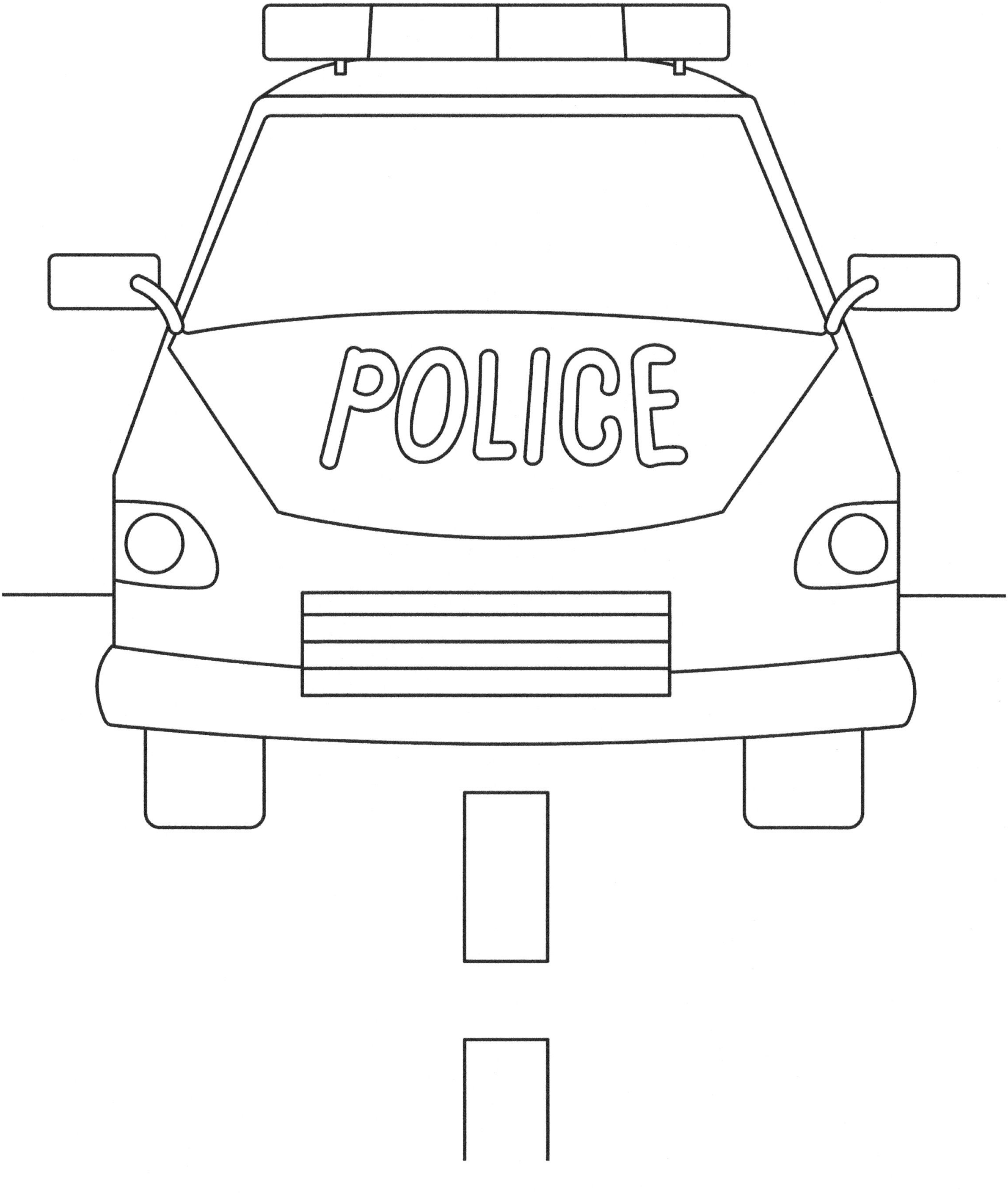
POLICE

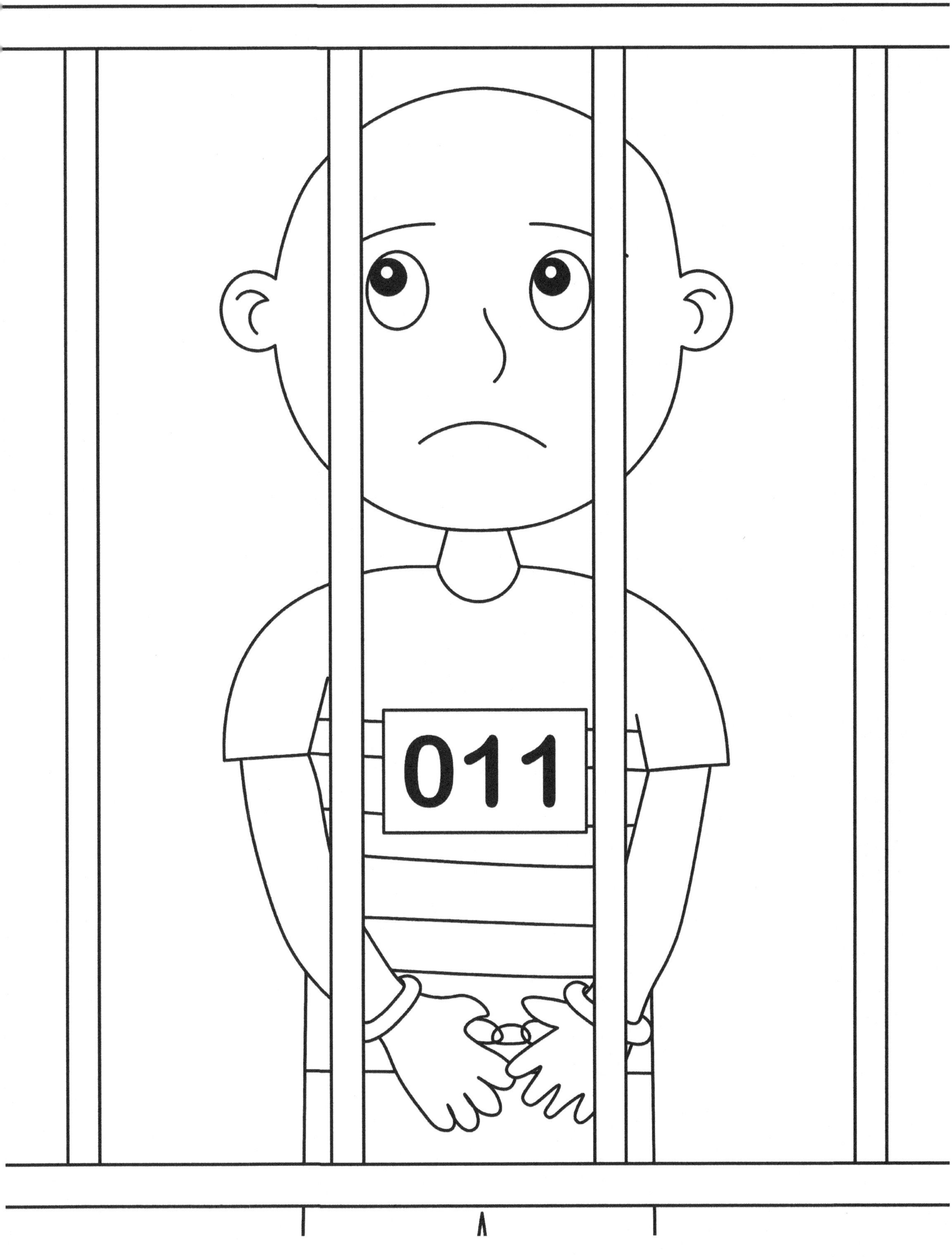
011

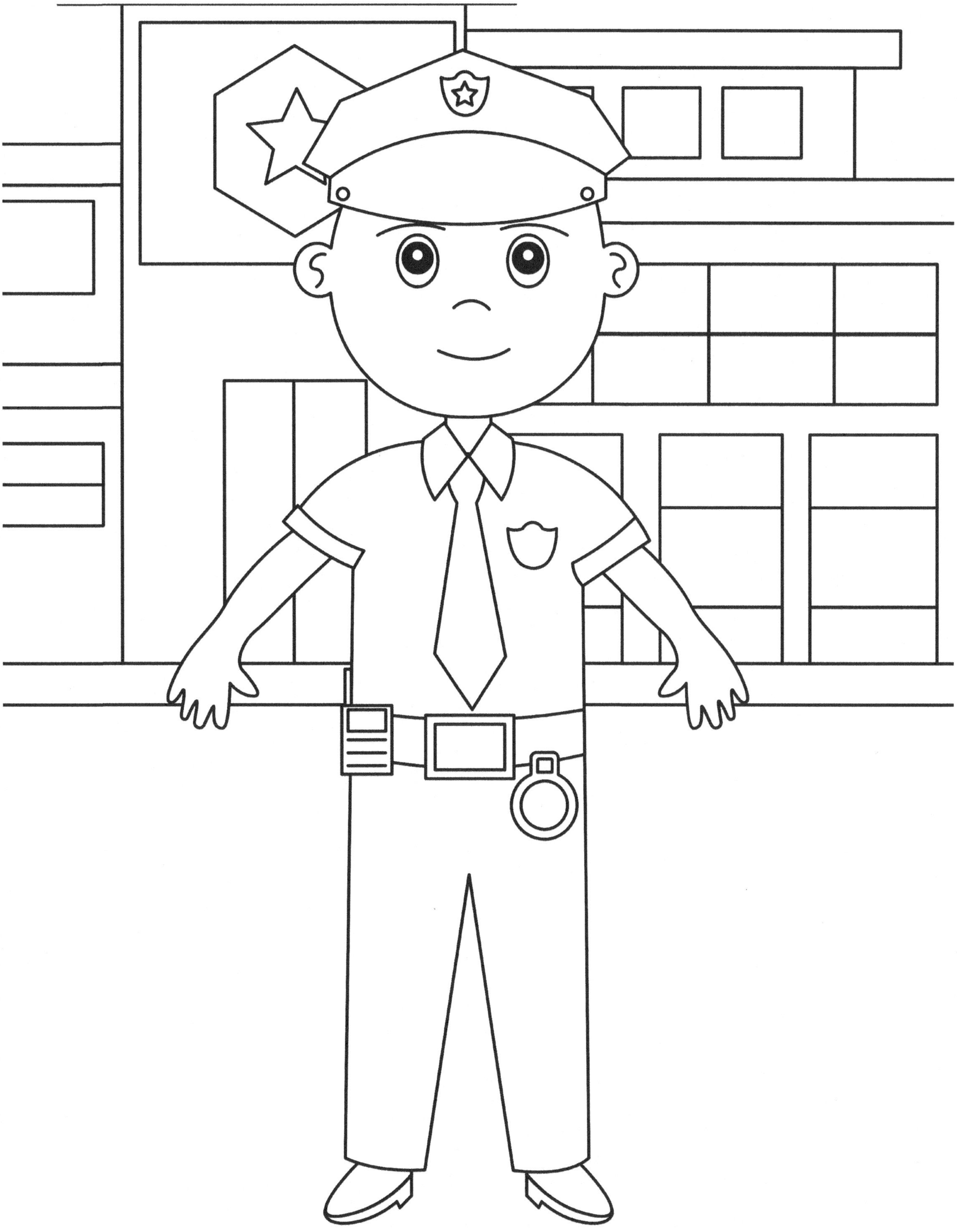

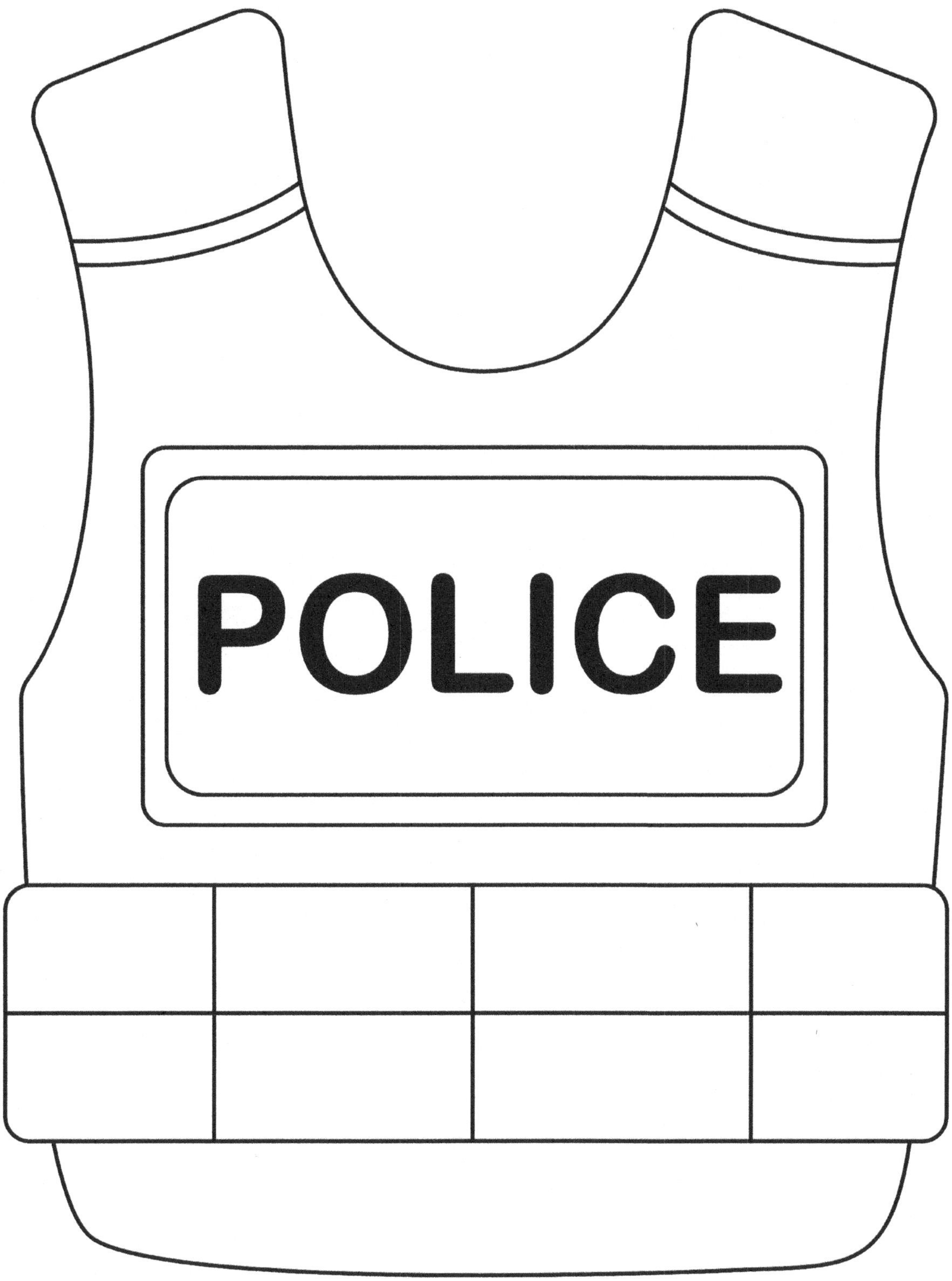
POLICE

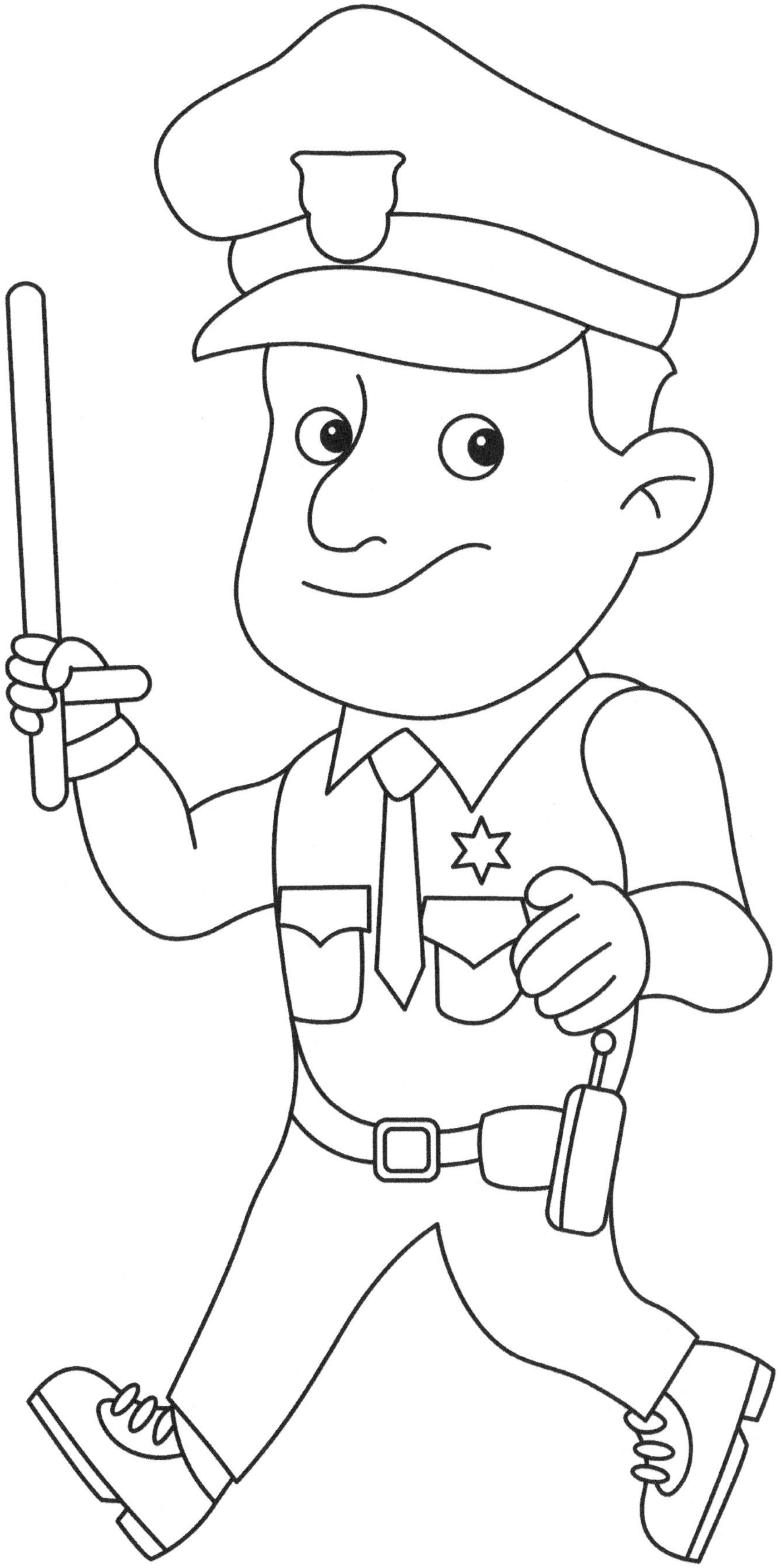

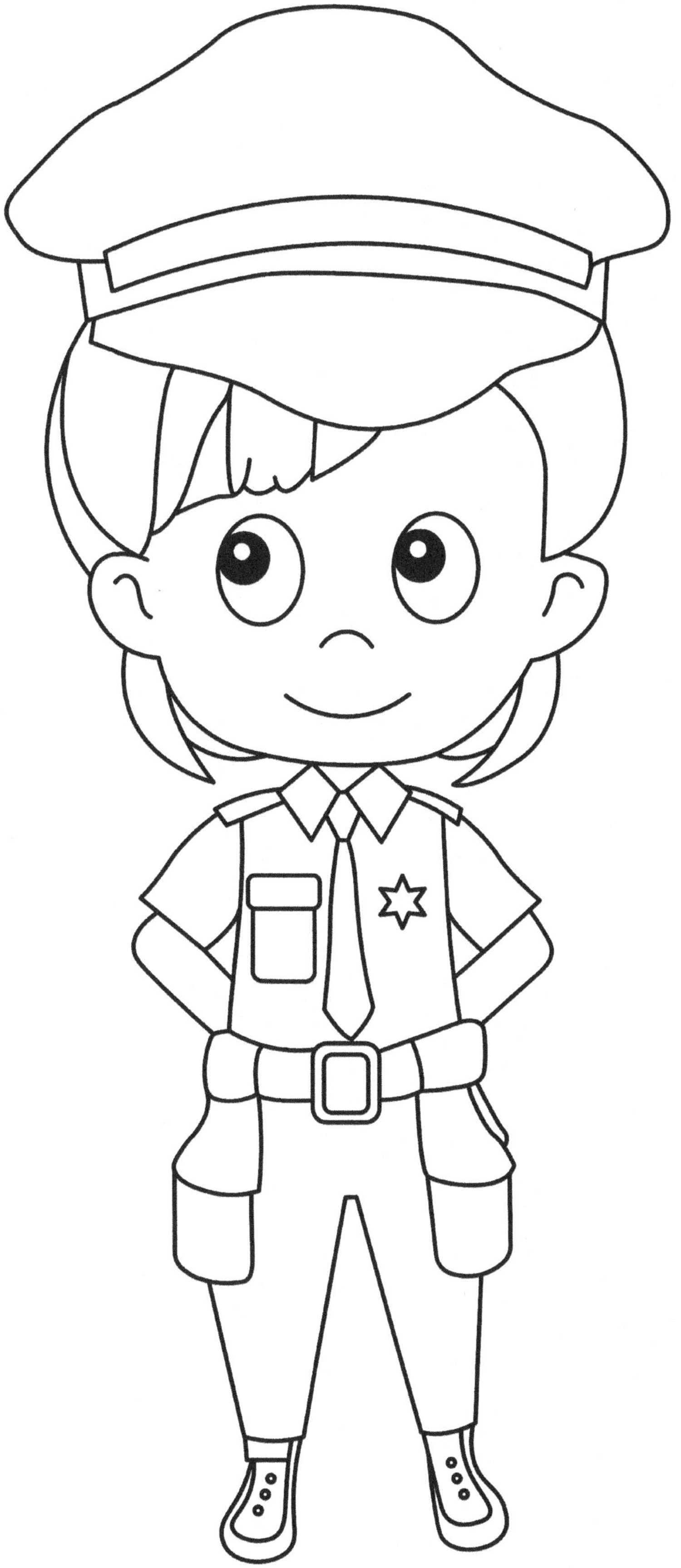

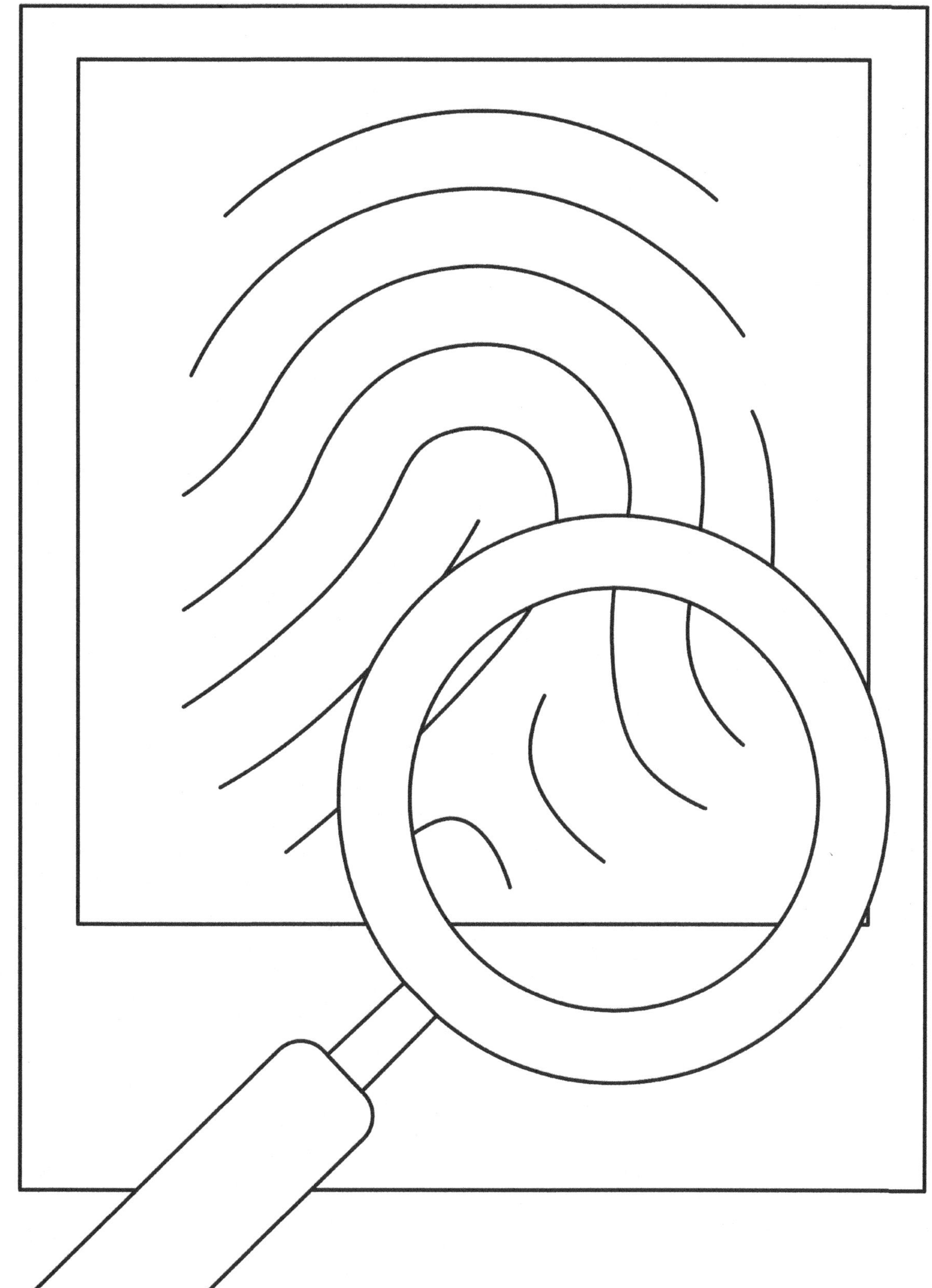

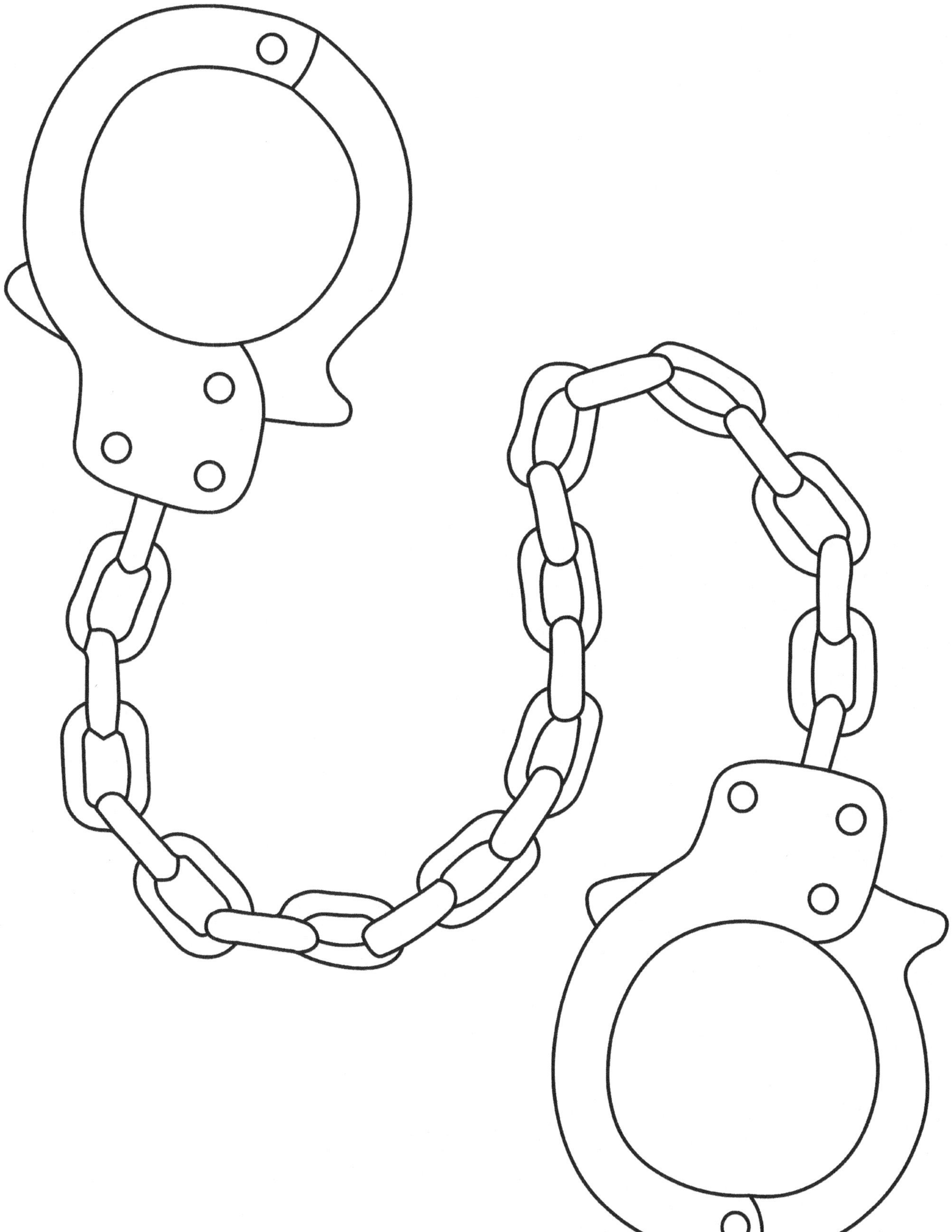

Made in the USA
Middletown, DE
12 June 2023

32489973R00031